INTRODUCING BIG BEN

Big Ben is a star - a personality - one of the most famous landmarks in the world - an instantly recognisable symbol of London, of England, and of the British. Although strictly speaking the name "Big Ben" refers only to the great hour bell, most people think of Big Ben as the whole thing - bell, clock, tower and chimes.

Big Ben was making news even before it was built and working, and even to this day it continues to command attention - Big Ben booms out over London and echoes across the Continents. It is a sound which has always suggested stability, safety and security to the British people. Big Ben announced the end of the First World War, and since then, on Armistice Day at 11am precisely, it signals the beginning of the two minutes' silence. And even during the Second World War, at the height of the bombing, Big Ben's deep, defiant tones could be heard on the nightly radio bulletin, often to the accompaniment of gunfire and sirens. The creation of Big Ben and the Clock Tower represented a tremendous feat of Victorian imagination, design and engineering, but it was certainly not a trouble-free operation. Not long before Big Ben started work as the capital's timekeeper in 1859, *The Times* wrote:

"The series of blunders and misconceptions, and misunderstandings, and squabbles respecting this clock are a disgrace to all concerned in it, and to the Government which permits them to go on."

Fortunately, since then, things have run smoothly and, apart from a rare hiccup, Big Ben has accurately marked the passage of time. This book tells the story of the design and history of this famous Clock Tower and bell. It is one of the major landmarks and buildings which, like Big Ben, are being restored to their original magnificence by the Property Services Agency (PSA).

I

Big Ben - the heartbeat of London.

THE COMPETITION AND THE CLOCK

The Clock Tower which now stands guard over the Palace of Westminster, alongside the River Thames, was built in the 1840s and 1850s. The previous building on the site was destroyed in a fire on Thursday, 16 October 1834, after two stokers piled up one of the furnaces and left it unattended. It caught fire and burned down most of the Palace. The news spread as quickly as the fire, and Londoners flocked in their thousands to watch as the flames engulfed the buildings. It raged through the night. Parliament decided to build itself a Gothic-style replacement on the same site, and in November 1835 a Commission was appointed to choose a design. In open competition 97 designs were submitted and the winner was Charles Barry. For the remaining 25 years of his life Barry had the difficult and often troublesome task of creating the new Palace which covers over eight acres of land.

A prominent feature of his final design was a clock tower. Barry was an accomplished architect but he knew little about clocks and bells. For advice and help he turned to his friend Benjamin Lewis Vulliamy, the Queen's clockmaker. Members of Parliament were becoming excited with the idea of the new clock which they had already titled "The Great Clock of Westminster." In an impassioned moment the Office of Works promised it would be "A noble clock, indeed a King of Clocks." Vulliamy, meanwhile, proceeded with his design. But, not surprisingly, other leading horologists, like E. J. Dent, were keen to compete for the honour of making this most important of clocks. Therefore, in 1846, the Commissioner decided to open it to limited competition. The Astronomer Royal, Sir George Airey, was appointed referee and proceeded to lay down 15 conditions. Two of these conditions demanded standards which had never been reached before:

- the first stroke of each hour had to be accurate to within one second;
- the clock's performance must be telegraphed twice a day to Greenwich Observatory for checking.

Airey's insistence on such high standards led to seven years of controversy, argument and delay. In need of an ally, Airey recruited Edmund Beckett Denison (later Baron Grimthorpe), a barrister and amateur clock designer, as his co-referee. Denison, who was later to take over the project single-handed, was extremely gifted, enormously ener-

Philadelphia Museum of Art: The John H. McFadden Collection

Above: The clock dial and upper part of the tower – from Sir Charles Barry's original proposed design.

Left: Burning of the Houses of Parliament, c. 1835 by J. M. W. Turner.

getic and almost universally unpopular, but his drive and determination contributed greatly to the eventual completion of Big Ben.

On 25 February 1852 the contract was finally awarded. For the sum of £1,800, E.J. Dent was to construct the clock according to Denison's own design. It was then discovered that the space in the tower would be too small for the clock. The architect, Charles Barry was blamed, but he replied that Denison should have checked the dimensions before designing the clock which had to be modified at a cost of £100.

The clock was finished in 1854 although it could not be installed because the Clock Tower was behind schedule. Thus for five years the clock's movement was kept on test at Dent's factory, allowing many improvements and refinements to be made. These included Denison's famous "Double Three-Legged Gravity Escapement," which has since become a standard feature in good public clocks. The escapement ensures that

Above: _Meeting of The Royal Fine Arts Commission, 1846_ by J. Partridge. The painting shows the architect, Barry, exhibiting a model of the Palace to the Commissioners.

Left: E.J. Dent – the scientific craftsman who manufactured the Great Clock.

Below: Sir Charles Barry (1795–1860) – the architect of the Palace of Westminster.

III

IV

outside influences such as wind pressure on the hands of the clock are not transmitted to the pendulum. By this means the time keeping is kept at a constant rate.

The pendulum itself is 13 feet long, weighs 6 cwt and beats every two seconds. On the pendulum rod is a small shelf on which there are a number of weights, including some pre-decimal pennies. So fine is the adjustment of this balance that the addition of one penny will cause the clock to gain two-fifths of a second in 24 hours. Twice weekly they are checked by the firm of Thwaites and Reed who took over responsibility for the clock from E.J. Dent & Co. Ltd. in 1971.

The bob of the pendulum weighs 4 cwt, the clock mechanism 5 tons, and the three clock weights total nearly 2½ tons. Until 1913 it took 30 man-hours a week to wind the clock mechanism, but now it is wound by electric motor. The clock began its life as London's official timekeeper on 31 May 1859.

P. Jackson

Opposite page: Controlled by coins. Pre-decimal pennies are used to regulate the clock's accuracy to the second. Twice a week it is checked – if the clock is gaining time a coin is taken off; if it is losing, a coin is added.

Left: Edmund Beckett Denison (1816–1905); later Baron Grimthorpe. Lawyer and amateur horologist, Denison designed the Great Clock.

Below: The clock mechanism under inspection.

V

MADE IN THE YEAR OF OUR

ENT, OF THE STRAND AND THE ROYAL EXCHANGE, CLOCKMAKER T

FIXED HERE

THE CLOCK TOWER

As the lower part of the new Clock Tower began to appear it must have seemed to the watching crowds as if it were being built by magic, because there was no external scaffolding. In fact the mighty tower was being constructed from the inside outwards.

Seated on a foundation of poured concrete 10 feet 1 inch thick, the Clock Tower stands 314 feet high from its base at river level to its finial at the top, and is about 40 feet square.

It is constructed of cast iron girders from the nearby Regents Canal Ironworks; Caen stone for the interior; Yorkshire Anston stone and Cornish granite for the exterior. The iron roofing plates came from a Birmingham foundry. The vast quantities of materials needed were brought mainly by river on lighters and canal barges, and landed on the adjoining wharves. Inside, a climbing scaffold enabled the materials to be lifted up the tower – a 2½ horsepower steam engine powered a winch which was mounted on iron rails and fixed to timber beams spanning the external walls from east to west. A travelling crane moved slowly round the rails, bringing materials up to the masons and bricklayers who worked from a platform slung below the main beams.

As work progressed the scaffolding was raised, 3½ feet at a time, by six giant screws. In all, it lifted 30,000 cubic feet of stone, 3,400 cubic yards of brickwork, and many tons of iron girders and plates. It was not used, however, to raise the bells themselves. In the west side of the tower, below the clock room, is a vertical air intake which was included for the ventilation of the main buildings. At one time a large furnace was kept burning at the base of the tower; the used or "vitiated" air from the Palace was funnelled into the Clock Tower, drawn up the shaft by the hot air and expelled out at the top. In the south-west corner is a stone staircase which serves all 11 floors. There are 334 steps from the ground floor to the belfry, and a further 59 steps to the lantern.

In the lower part of the tower, a third of the way up, is the room which was intended as a prison cell for offenders from both Houses. In the nineteenth century, the Serjeant-at-Arms could be directed by the Speaker of the House of Commons to detain those Members who were rude or noisy during debates. Officially a Member could be detained for what was left of a parliamentary session, which might have amounted to a number of months. In practice, however, no one suffered the shame for more than a day. It was last used in 1880 when Charles Bradlaugh refused to take the oath of allegiance to Queen Victoria. He was sentenced to one night's custody in the Clock Tower cell, which in fact was a quite comfortable room.

Left: Under construction with no sign of scaffolding. The Clock Tower was actually built from the inside outwards.

Below: Charles Bradlaugh in the Clock Tower's prison room. In 1880, Bradlaugh, an MP, was imprisoned overnight for refusing to take the oath of allegiance.

Opposite page: The delicate Gothic tracery of the Clock Tower – after decades of dirt had been removed.

VII

VIII

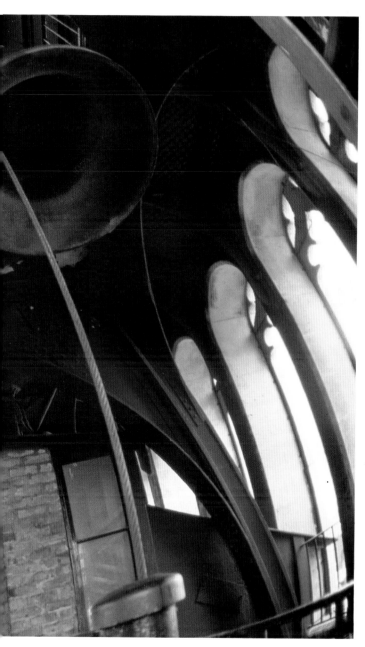

THE WESTMINSTER CHIMES.

1ST QUARTER.

2ND QUARTER.

3RD QUARTER.

HOUR

IX

All through this hour   Lord, be my guide   And by Thy power

No foot shall slide

X

THE CLOCK FACE

The richest decoration of the Tower is in the clock storey and above. In designing this part of the building Sir Charles Barry was greatly influenced by Augustus Welby Pugin.

Within the clock storey, projecting beyond the walls of the tower, sit the famous clock faces. They each measure 23 feet in diameter and are made of cast iron. Originally they were glazed with a German double flashed opal glass. However, subsequent repairs at various times using English glass produced a peculiar grey and white patchwork effect. So in 1956, during repairs and overhaul, all four faces were reglazed with a Birmingham-made pot opal glass. Each face contains 312 separate pieces of glass.

The minute spaces on the dials are each 1 foot square and the hour figures are 2 feet long. One unusual feature of this clock is that the hour figure of four o'clock is indicated by the Roman IV, rather than the usual IIII. The minute hands are made of copper sheet, hollowed and fashioned to shape. They are 14 feet long, weigh 2 cwt each, and travel over 100 miles a year at their tips. The hour hands are of gun-metal, weigh 6 cwt each and are 9 feet long.

Behind the clock faces run galleries from where the dials are illuminated. Until 1900, lighting was supplied by a number of gas jets fitted with large Bray burners. After electricity was installed the dials were lit by ordinary tungsten light until 1957 when it was replaced by cold cathode lighting. Today, each face is illuminated by 28 tubes which total 10,000 candle power.

In the lantern above the belfry is another light – the Ayrton Light, named after Acton Smee Ayrton, a First Commissioner. Since 1885 this light has signalled that Parliament was at work.

It was a dark day for London and the world when, on 1 September 1939, the clock lights were extinguished to conform with war-time black-out regulations. But at the end of the war in Europe, on 30 April 1945, a very different atmosphere was in evidence. At 10.15 pm, to the delight of the cheering crowds gathered below in Parliament Square, the Speaker of the House threw a switch and the lights of the clock faces once again shone out over London.

Under each face there is a Latin inscription carved in the stone: *Domine salvam fac reginam nostram Victoriam primam.* The work of Pugin, who used the phrase extensively in his decoration of the new Palace, it is a prayer for the Queen from the Catholic Latin mass and means:
"O Lord, save our Queen Victoria the First."

Royal Institute of British Architects

Opposite page: One of the most famous faces in the world – the Great Clock of Westminster.

Above: Augustus Welby Pugin (1812–52). Pugin contributed a great deal to the design and decoration of the Clock Tower.

Below: Behind the dial – 23 feet in diameter, each face contains 312 separate pieces of Birmingham-made pot opal glass.

BIG BEN - THE BELL

Above: Method of making the bell mould.

Below: The bell was taken to London by ship and pulled across Westminster Bridge by 16 white horses.

Few people, hearing the thunderous sounds of Big Ben, will imagine the troubled history of that great bell.

It was first cast on 6 August 1856 at Warner's of Norton, near Stockton-on-Tees. At 16 tons it was the biggest ever cast in the country. By rail it went to West Hartlepool, to be shipped to London. It was dropped on to the deck of the schooner, badly damaging the ship, and was then nearly lost at sea in a storm. On arrival at the Port of London it was placed on a specially built carriage and pulled across Westminster Bridge by 16 white horses. Hung on gallows in New Palace Yard it was tested each day throughout 1857.

When it arrived the bell's official name was Victoria although this was quickly forgotten in favour of "Big Ben". There are two theories of how the bell got this name: the first suggests that it was taken from the nickname of a champion heavyweight boxer of the time called Ben Caunt; the second and more probable explanation is that it was named after the bulky Welshman, Sir Benjamin Hall, who was First Commissioner of Works from 1855 to 1858 and whose name was inscribed on the bell.

BBC Hulton Picture Library

In October 1857 disaster struck during the testing - a 4 foot long crack appeared in the bell. This produced a flurry of accusations and arguments. Some blamed the composition of the bell metal; others claimed the waist of the bell was too thick. Warner's said it was due to the weight of the bell's clapper which Denison had increased from 7 cwt to 13 cwt.

Whatever the cause the bell had to be broken up and recast. This time Warner's asked too high a price, so the job was done by George Mears at the Whitechapel Foundry in London, on 10 April 1858.

In October 1858 the new bell, 9 feet in diameter, 7½ feet in height and 3 tons lighter than the first version, was ready to be installed. But there was another snag - the mouth of the bell was too wide to go up the shaft of the tower. Then someone had an ingenious idea - the bell was turned on its side and winched up in a cradle. It took teams of men 30 hours to raise it to the belfry, where it was suspended from massive iron girders. By this time the four quarter bells, which had been cast at Warner's Crescent Foundry in London, were in place, ready to accompany Big Ben in the Westminster Chimes.

But even then there were more problems with the bell and the clock. Firstly, the clock would not go - it was discovered that the cast-iron minute hands were too heavy, so they

were replaced by lighter copper ones. Then, when Big Ben eventually started service as a striking clock on 11 July 1859, MPs immediately complained it was too loud.

P. Jackson

XIII

P. Jackson

Worse was to follow. In September of that year the bell cracked again. For the next three years Big Ben was silent and the hour had to be struck on the fourth quarter bell.

Finally, in 1862 the Astronomer Royal found a cure; the bell was turned by a quarter turn so that it was struck on a different spot; a small

square was cut out to prevent the crack from spreading, and the weight of the hammer was reduced from 6½ cwt to 4 cwt. Once again Big Ben rang out, as it does to this day.

The total cost of making the clock and bells and putting them in the tower was £22,000 by 1859.

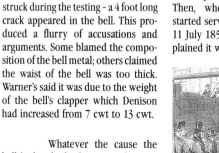

The Illustrated London News Picture Library

Above: A specially made chain, nearly 1,800 feet long, was used to hoist the Great Bell, in October 1858. Due to its enormous size, the bell had to be turned on its side and winched up in a cradle.

Top right: Ben Caunt, the heavyweight boxer nicknamed "Big Ben" who, some believe, may have inspired the bell's name.

Centre right: In October 1857, while being tested in New Palace Yard, Big Ben cracked. Broken up, it was recast at the Whitechapel Bell Foundry in London.

Bottom right: In 1859, after it had finally been raised up the Clock Tower, the bell cracked again and could not be used. Three years later the problem was solved when the bell was given a quarter turn.

Time takes its toll, even on great timekeepers, and maintenance of the Parliament buildings is vitally important. It was in 1934 when the Clock Tower last received a wash and facelift to repair the damage caused by years of soot, smog and pigeons. The ironwork of the dials was cleaned and painted, and the stonework surrounding them was painted and gilded.

In 1956 the clock and bell chamber received a much needed overhaul after the buffeting inflicted during the war.

Then, in 1981, the authorities decided it was time for another complete overhaul. Maintenance of the Palace of Westminster is the responsibility of the Property Services Agency.

The restoration of the Clock Tower and clock face was part of a massive 6.5 million pound cleaning and restoration programme - managed by the PSA - for the entire Palace of Westminster. It should be completed by the end of the decade. The work on the Clock Tower began in 1983, was completed in 1985, cost approximately 1.7 million pounds, and won the PSA the 1986 City of Westminster 'Heritage Award'.

To reach the top of the tower took 130,000 feet of scaffolding, and repairs to the stonework required 105 cubic feet of Clipsham Stone from Rutland quarries. Some repairs were also needed to the ironwork. The regilding of decorated surfaces used 4,000 books of gold leaf. The dismantling of the clock was some feat: the 14 feet long minute hands and the 9 feet long hour hands all had to be removed so that their bearings could be replaced.

XIV

Far left: Each minute hand is 14 feet long and travels the equivalent of 100 miles per year.

Left: The restoration programme used Sir Charles Barry's description in his Illustrations of the New Palace of Westminster, Second Series *published in 1865, as reference for the decoration.*

Opposite page: 4,000 books of gold leaf were used during the restoration.

The PSA had problems with the decoration of the carving surrounding the clock faces. On the repainting they sought advice from the Historic Buildings and Monuments Commission, but there was a distinct lack of documentary reference on this subject. For although most of the red, green, blue and gold design was known, in his description of the New Palace of Westminster, the architect, Sir Charles Barry had omitted to state the colour of the metalwork surrounding the dial.

So the Commission had to do some detective work: having taken five examples of paint from the ogee, or "S" shaped moulding, below the dials, they discovered that the two most recent schemes were black. Other samples, taken from one of the letters of the Latin inscription beneath the dial, revealed layers of white, red, white again, deep cream, gold size and gold leaf.

Above: 130,000 feet of scaffolding were needed to reach the top of the tower.

Left: As good as new – one of the ornamental shields above the belfry.

Right: The restoration work began in 1983 and was completed in 1985.

The Commissioners advised that two shades of blue should now be used, but the Secretary of State felt that as the black scheme had been known to most people since 1934, and is frequently seen by the public on television, then it should remain black.

On Wednesday 5 June 1985, Mr Speaker, the Rt. Hon. Bernard Weatherill MP performed a ceremony at the south clock face, when he tightened the nut holding the clock hands in position. This signified the unveiling of all four faces of the great clock which had been hidden from its public by scaffolding and plastic sheeting for 30 months during its restoration.

The London air is much cleaner today than it was 50 years ago, and in all probability the Clock Tower and Big Ben will not need another major overhaul for at least 75 years.